Life.

Andrea Brown

BookLeaf Publishing

Life, Love, Loss © 2023 Andrea Brown

All rights reserved.

No part of this publication may be reproduced, stored in a retrieval system, or transmitted, in any form or by any means, electronic, mechanical, photocopying, recording or otherwise, without the prior written permission of the presenters.

Andrea Brown asserts the moral right to be identified as author of this work.

Presentation by *BookLeaf Publishing*

Web: www.bookleafpub.com

E-mail: info@bookleafpub.com

ISBN: 9789357446044

First edition 2023

To my siblings for supporting me in my creativity and my madness.

PREFACE

This book was put together as part of the 21 day poetry challenge. Some of the work has been hastily thrown together. But sometimes that's the best way, right?

Beautiful Day

There was silence as I made my way
Through the field and into the woods
Nothing to see here, nobody around
But myself, my thoughts, my mood
Sunlight shines through the branches of trees
Like golden lasers twinkling in my way
Those sparkling projections are soothing for my soul
It is such a beautiful day

A flock of wood pigeons in the field
Startle as they sense my presence
En masse, they abandon their meeting spot
And I wonder where it is they are heading
I walk across the freshly ploughed field
I look down to the soft brown soil and I stare
I see small, shiny fragments of glass and china
And I wonder how they came to be there

I pick up a stone that is mottled and pink
And admire its colours, how it feels in my palm
And I wonder why this gives me such comfort
When I feel it in my pocket and in my hand
I look around me in wonder and awe
Nature has given me a wonderful display
A unique performance just for me alone
It truly is a beautiful day

If Only

I wish

The laziest of sentiments

If you want something so badly

Then make it happen

If only

Regrets are futile

It's done, move on

You can't change what has been

I want

Then do it

Don't waste time dreaming

Make it happen

I love

Then treasure that feeling

That is never a given

Or guaranteed to last

Just As You Are

A lion doesn't tell you that it's a lion
Your actions should describe who you are
You don't need to broadcast your edited highlights
And how are adored by those near and far
Is it that you feel insecure
And need constant reassurance of your worth?
That you are wanted, needed and loved
That you have a reason to be on this Earth?
Whatever you are, let your actions describe you
A running commentary is not required
You don't need to tell everyone what you are
If you are loved, respected and admired

Crazy

You told me I was the only one
We were meant to be, you and I
You told me that you loved me
I think you fucking lied

You said it was forever
But time just wasn't on our side
You said we could have been for keeps
Another fucking lie

I'd keep my phone in my hand all night
But it simply won't comply
I keep checking that it's not on silent - it isn't
I feel like I want to die

Did you ever need me
The way that I wanted you to?
You said the words I wanted to hear
But you didn't mean them, did you?

But nevertheless I'd still have followed you
To the ends of the Earth if I must
No matter what I was drowning
In a sea of obsession and lust
Waves of emotion buried me

Knocking me over, pushing me underneath
I couldn't keep myself from loving you
I'll admit, through gritted teeth

But I cannot live my life like this
Waiting for you and wondering why
And though it breaks my heart, I know
That we must say a final goodbye

I love you and that will never change
But I will never be your leading lady
I've played a bit part in the story of your life
And it made me fucking crazy

Done

Drowning
That's how it feels
I am underwater, can't breathe
Each intake of breath sends me deeper

Suffocating
There is oxygen
But no matter how my lungs expand
I don't feel like I am breathing

Sick
I am sick of the lies
Spewing from my mouth
And yours too

Done
I am done with this
I am worth more
And you are too

Everything To Me

Don't ever feel unworthy
Undeserving of my love
Don't think that you are nothing
You will never be enough
My heart wants you to realise
But you just refuse to see
That I'm desperately in love with you
And you mean everything to me

From sunrise to sunset and the hours in between
And when darkness fills the sky each night
I see you in my dreams
You are never far from my thoughts
I only wish that you could see
That my heart belongs to you, my love
And you mean everything to me

Unrequited Love

I touch your skin as I wish you would mine

Cup my hands round your sweet face

I kiss your lips and taste you now

Drinking in your scent as we embrace

I am seeing a different side of me

And I'm not sure that I like it

I am desperate, obsessive and jealous

Although I try my best to hide it

I don't want to be this person

Chasing an impossible dream

On the outside I play my usual part

But inside there is a silent scream

My love for you is all consuming

All I think about is you

And in a different lifetime

You would feel the same about me too

The Girl Who Wasn't Enough

Teardrops fall
And that's not all

What she feels inside
Is pain
And shame

The hopelessness, the loneliness
Would it ever ever subside?

Her heart was on the floor
She wanted to be so much more
But life was just too tough

For in her mind she would always be
The girl who wasn't enough

Let Them

Let them talk
If it gives them a sense of importance
They might feel good about themselves
For a short while at least

Let them gossip
If it gives them a thrill
To shock each other
With tales of your misdoings

Let them laugh
For laughter is healthy, right?
Even if it is
At your expense

Let them hate
For anyone who feels this strongly
Does not deserve
To take up your thoughts

Let them love
If they love you truly they wont indulge
Instead they will choose to ignore or defend you
Keep them close. They are the only ones worth
your time.

Keep Walking

People stare as I walk past
I can hear them talking
I care not for their opinions
I just keep on walking

If I can walk fast enough
The colour will return to my face
So I put my head down, take a deep breath
And I pick up the pace

My life may be falling apart right now
Thoughts in my head are truly shocking
But I refuse to look back or have any regrets
Instead I will just keep on walking

Because I'm Worth It

Don't give me your opinion
It is meaningless to me
What you see and what I am
Are different you see
You think that you can read me
Well think again my friend
You couldn't be more in the wrong
I have nothing to defend
It is easy to find fault with me
If you look hard enough
I wonder if you look at yourself
And criticise as much
Whatever, I'll still carry on
Regardless of your shit
Always keeping in my mind
That I'm most definitely worth it

Sorry

Sorry
The hardest word to say
But the most powerful that will pass your lips
Not an admission of guilt
But the purest form of empathy
Recognising the hurt
Not seeking to apportion blame
But to acknowledge the feelings of others
The hurt, the sorrow, the anger
And when you have mastered this
You are a human of the highest order

Ugly Voice

There's an ugly voice inside my head
Who tells me he doesn't believe
I don't have the strength to argue with him
Today nothing will be achieved

'You must be such a fool
To think you could ever succeed'
The voice whispers in my ear
And I whisper back 'Agreed'

And at every turn, the results of my efforts
Would seem to prove him right
I'm like King Midas but instead of gold
Everything I touch turns to shite

Today has been a bad day
Congratulations ugly voice, you have won
But tomorrow will be different, wait and see
Tomorrow I'll get shit done

I will silence your negativity
Remind myself you're not real
Your voice is only my own self belief
A crappy reflection of how I feel

I need to change the voice in my head
To the voices of people I love
Who have shown me warmth and kindness
And when needed, a gentle shove

So to my ugly thoughts, yes today was your day
And I allowed that, it was my choice
But tomorrow, the beautiful choir in my head
Will sing 'Fuck right off, ugly voice'

Baby Blues

The first time that I saw her
I shed the first of many tears
I thought I would feel a rush of love
But all I felt was fear

I had waited so long for this moment
I thought I was prepared
But now, here with my babe in arms
All I felt was scared

Ten perfect little fingers and toes
Eyes so big and blue
I had read all the mother and baby books
But still didn't know what to do

This wasn't what I expected
But what I did not know
Was a seed of love had been planted
And it was going to grow

My baby's getting older now
And I love her more each day
Beginning to enjoy motherhood
Now the fear has gone away

There is no doubt about it
Motherhood is tough
But you don't need to be perfect at it
'Good Enough' is good enough

Looking at my little one now
Makes everything worthwhile
As I look back on the early days
I look forward with a smile

A Year Ago Today

Life as I knew it turned upside down
A year ago today
I never thought that losing you
Would change me in this way
A year ago today
I was looking after you
Little did I appreciate then
How much you supported me too
Every little achievement
I would share – good news and bad
We spent so many hours putting the world to rights
Oh how I miss you Dad
I know I didn't always make you proud
Though those words were never spoken
But in later years we grew so close
Formed a bond that wouldn't be broken
A year ago today
It was time to say goodbye
It wasn't how I imagined it would be
But the time had come, we couldn't deny
So today I'm thinking of you Dad
But that is nothing new
We said goodbye a year ago today
And life will never be the same without you

Broken

I see you in my dreams each night

But awaken forever alone

When I close my eyes and see your face

My heart can't accept you are gone

I thought I saw you yesterday, as I often do

Chased a stranger down the street because they looked like you

It's madness I know, but I still hold onto the thought

That it was just a dream and you're still here

My heart just can't cope that you're not

And how I move on is unclear

I will never be the same person again

When you died, part of me did too

I am sullen and bitter, I hate everyone

I have no time for anyone, since I lost you

I am asked how I am as a courtesy, how I really feel is unspoken

My dreams and my mind tell me every day

That I am truly broken

Missing You At Christmas

Missing you at Christmas
Just like every other day
Festivities and good wishes
Seem hollow since you went away
I wish that I could write to you
Not to spread Christmas cheer
But just to say that with all my heart
I wish that you were here
But life doesn't last forever
And when your time had come
We knew we had to let you go
Your work here it was done
Thinking back tonight to Christmasses past
And loved ones we still miss
I'll look up at the sky tomorrow
And blow you all a Christmas kiss

Without You

Ripples on the water
going round inside my mind
No matter how you want to
You can't turn back the time

My body aches with sadness
My heart broken in two
I was just so unprepared
For a life without you

3 Sides to Every Story - COVID and General Practice

The patient

I have called 320 times today
Look at my phone and you'll see
But when I come into the practice
The waiting room's empty

Don't tell me you're still seeing patients
Like the rest of the NHS do
You're hiding in your rooms all day
Maybe making a phone call or two

I just want to have an appointment
With a GP, face to face
You can't give me what I want over the phone
Your system is a disgrace

I don't want to tell the receptionist
What the problem is
She is not a Doctor
It's none of her business

It's simple - why don't you just get more GPs?
Make it like it used to be again
If you had enough Doctors here
I'd have no reason to complain

The Receptionist

I travel to work each morning
Dreading what today will bring
With no appointments left come ten past eight
Abuse is a regular thing

We feel the brunt of folk's anger
And are seen as being in the way
When they can't get to speak to their GP
On any given day

The patients are reluctant to share with us
Any information – which is a shame
We may have been able to help them ourselves
By signposting like we've been trained

Many of the patients
Who have booked a slot today
Could have easily treated themselves at home
Or gone to the pharmacy

One episode of diarrhoea
Or a sore throat since yesterday
Takes GPs away from the genuinely unwell
But we can't turn them away

I wish that they would realise
That we are human too
The daily abuse when we can't meet demand
We shouldn't have to suffer this – would you?

The GP

We've never been 'in hiding'
I hate this negative press
We are working harder than ever before
And always doing our best

We have had to change the way we worked
To keep our patients safe
More telephone appointments, virtual consultations
But we do still see patients face to face

Listening to the media
It's no wonder we can't recruit GPs
Who would want to come into a profession
Where you're the subject of such hostility

The truth is we just can't provide
The service our patients desire
But at the very least we try to deliver
The basic care they require

I wish that people would realise
We aren't lazy and we do care
We still want to do our very best
But we are burnt out and we are scared

We would love to have capacity
To go over and above for you all
But the truth is there aren't enough of us here
And I don't see this changing at all

Why Do I Do It?

'What do you do?' I am often asked
'A Practice Manager, you say?
So what exactly does that entail
On any given day?'

Well.....

HR, health and safety, recruitment and retention
IT, training and development, too many emails
to mention
Budgets and schedules, rotas, complaints
All fitted in around tight time constraints

Supporting all my colleagues
Who are struggling to cope
Meetings, moans and merriment
Lunch break – that's a joke!

But despite it all I wouldn't change
I know I was destined for this
I once dreamed of being where I am now
And I'll hold onto that wish

My Door is Always Open

All the best managers will say

'My door is always open'

Always ready for interruptions

To fix whatever is broken

But let's take a step back and re-think this

What this means to others

Is I don't value my own time

Like, 'Come on in, it's really no bother'

No matter what I am doing

I will drop everything for you

My door is always open

But would yours be open for me too?

Milton Keynes UK
Ingram Content Group UK Ltd.
UKHW020711050923
428087UK00018B/1428

9 789357 446044